PACT to Go

Rod and Ruthie Gilbert

PACT to go
Revised 2020 Edition

Copyright @ Rod & Ruthie Gilbert
Email: r2gilberto@fastmail.fm

Published by:
Elemental Publishing LLC
PO Box 79
Niceville, FL 32588
info@elementalpub.com

ISBN: 978-1-935614-16-6

Cover Design By Luke Gilbert

Printed In USA For World Wide Distribution (excluding India)

Unless otherwise specified, all Scripture quotations are taken from, New International version copyright© 1978 by New York International Bible Society.

For more copies write to :

PO Box 79
Niceville, FL 32588

Dedication

We dedicate this book to present and future cross-cultural workers, of all nations, and in particular to those who stirred our hearts in their personal visits to Cornerstone House in South India, to Bethany Ministries in Hong Kong, and now to the Old Mill, Kingsnorth in Kent.

Acknowledgements

Our heartfelt thanks go to our dear friends Ross and Christine Paterson and to the many who work with them inside and outside of China whose lives have also contributed to this message. Ross and Christine have given their time sacrificially way beyond just the words. They bring their huge wealth of insight and understanding of mission, along with their passion to see people survive and thrive in their calling in the Great Commission.

To our own PACTeam, introduced through the pages of this book, to whom we owe a huge debt of gratitude in modelling the PACTeam principles so effectively and who have so self-sacrificially shared their lives with us.

To all those who have contributed to the contents of this book, too many to enumerate, but often named or referred to in the text. We thank all of them for being so willing to share their lives.

To Brad and Paige Hudson of Elemental Publishers, who have so generously given of their expertise in enabling this book to be available to anyone, anywhere.

Rod and Ruthie Gilbert
Kingsnorth, Kent 2019

Table of Contents

Foreword

Christine Paterson

It was that phone call that every parent must dread to receive. It was 5.30 in the morning and we were at home in Singapore, when the bedside phone shocked us awake. Sleepily, Ross reached out to pick up the receiver. "Hello Dad, is that you?" Our second daughter, Hannah, was calling from Dubai where she was taking part in a mission trip "I just heard that Debs has been in a car crash outside Cambridge... they are operating now". Hannah was uncertain of the details, but she had just learned that her sister, our firstborn, was seriously injured. As we were soon to find out, she was not expected to live. In God's mercy, our beautiful daughter's life was spared, and she eventually made a full recovery, though for many hours it was touch and go. Others stood in for us at the bedside till we could get home.

This is one of many crises, of various proportions, that have hit us over a lifetime of serving in missions. It highlights how hard it can be to be thousands of miles away when a crisis occurs in the home country, and how much one needs folk who can be called upon to help. Our support group in Cheltenham was alerted to pray, while my brother and nephew drove immediately to the hospital to identify her and 'be there' for us. We later discovered that thousands round the world had joined in the prayer circle, as the news about Debs and her passenger, Sophie, spread virally across the Internet. We were immensely grateful for all who stood with us and with our family throughout that time.

Oswald J Smith, the famous pastor from Toronto of a bygone time said:

> *"Suppose a child should fall into a well, who would get the reward for the child's rescue, the one who held the rope and lowered the other to the bottom, or both? God says they will share alike. The one who stands at the top and makes it possible for the other to go down into the well in order that the child might be rescued is just as much entitled to the reward as the one who goes down. You may not be able to go down; you may never see the foreign field, but you can hold the rope. You can make it possible for someone else to go. You can send a substitute, and if you do, your reward will be just as great as the reward of those who actually go..."*

Smith then goes on to use another metaphor, this time from old-time fire fighting, which sheds further light on the teamwork involved:

*"Everyone must be in the bucket brigade. You
may not be the one who throws the water
on the fire at the end of the line, you may be
somewhere in the centre passing the bucket, or
you may be dipping up the water. The question
is: are you in the line? Do you belong to the
bucket brigade? Are you doing something –
praying maybe?" (Oswald J. Smith)*

What, then, is the concept here? Essentially, that sending people to share the gospel in another culture is only part of what it takes to be obedient to what we call 'The Great Commission'. The other part of the equation is that those who go out need to find others who will team up with them back home, to help them thrive, not just survive, over there for the long haul. That is what this small book is about. Although pastors, agency leaders, and even ordinary church members, will find much to think through in this book, the primary focus is not so much on what **they** should do to support cross-cultural workers. It is more about what those who go out can do for **themselves** to raise up a team that is committed specifically to supporting them.

Usually, our best supporters are our own personal friends. Since these are unlikely to be from one church, it follows that the supporting team we are talking about will not be 'under' any one church either. It will grow up organically around us, and may change strategically over time, based on different the stages and seasons through that we all go in a lifetime of service to Jesus.

Ross and I have had varied experience in terms of support in our life in missions. Ross started out by going alone as a single man to work in Taiwan in 1969.

He only had one supporting church behind him, but he had a strong call from God to serve the Chinese. He went in faith that God would open the door of service, which He wonderfully and progressively did. Ross was from a non-Christian background, so even from that point of view he was rather 'on his own'. I, on the other hand, had been raised on the 'field' – my parents worked in missions in Central Africa for over forty years. While I had rebelled ferociously in my early teens, I had come back to the Lord quite dramatically in my final year at school, and soon after that went up to York University. I met Ross when he was 'adviser' to the Christian Union I joined there, just a few months before he left for Taiwan. Our courtship was complicated, separated as we were by thousands of miles, but we eventually married in 1975, and I joined him in Taiwan for a further 4 years. Debs was born there in 1978.

It was, bizarrely, in Africa later that year, while bringing our newborn to meet her grandparents, that we had our first encounter with mainland Chinese people, just as their nation was opening up again, after thirty years of being cut off from the outside world. Three young men from NE China, with whom we shared the gospel quite freely in their language, confirmed God's leading to us: "You must come to our country", they said, "Our people all need to hear this good news!". That marked a switch in direction, and in one way or another, we have been serving the church and the people of that great nation ever since. After ten years of living and working in Asia, the next fourteen years, much to our surprise, were spent in the north of England, where four more wonderful daughters were born to us and where the China work began. For thirteen years after that, we served from Singapore and since 2007 from Taiwan once again. Our mandate from the beginning was to raise awareness about China and to "provide for her church's nurture and growth". That has included training and sending and caring for others of many nationalities who have joined us over the years.

We first met Rod and Ruthie when Rod was headmaster at Hebron School in South India. It was 1995, and by then we had moved to Singapore with our family. All our plans for our children's education had gone 'pear-shaped', as they say, and we were desperate! However Rod did the impossible, and managed to take in all five daughters in the middle of the school year! We quickly came to love and respect them both. Then, as our two families got to know each other, we became fast friends, who have had more than a few 'roller-coaster rides of faith' together.

Time went by, and Rod and Ruthie moved on from Hebron to work again in Scripture Union (SU) India. They started a family ministry and established Cornerstone House near Chennai, where they also wrote the book '*Marriage Masala – 52 spices for a healthy marriage*', and a curriculum, which became the basis of training others to do marriage ministry. Rod also took up the regional directorship of SU South Asia. After that they went to Sri Lanka for four years, as Rod had been 'headhunted' to be Principal of Trinity College, Kandy. Seeking to return this prestigious school to its Christian roots and unaligned foundation (in the peak of the civil war), he stirred up some hornets' nests and met strong resistance to change. Ultimately this resulted in their being deported, with risk to their very lives – that story will also be referred to in the book.

For two years after leaving Sri Lanka, they were based at Bethany Ministries in Hong Kong on Cheung Chau Island – a place where mission workers can go for rest and refreshment. There they worked first hand with hundreds of people of all nationalities who had a passion for mission, a number of whom had come close to burn out. And these days, now based in the UK, they are still hosting and mentoring families and young people from all over the world in their homestead of Kingsmill, Kent, with the strapline of 'wide open spaces' (Romans 5:2 *The Message*). All this cross-cultural, pastoral involvement has merely underscored to them that part of the 'missing link' in long term effectiveness in mission and good member care is what we call in this book a 'PACTeam'.

Rod and Ruthie have the most developed and effective PACTeam we have ever seen, so what is written here comes from their very practical and valuable experience. For us personally, their move to Bethany in Hong Kong provided us with more opportunities to serve together. They graciously gave us input with Member Care in our organisation and shared with our members the principles of this book, on how to build up and sustain their own PACTeams. Ross and I are also very supportive on the concept. We have built out own team whom we value highly, and we hope that this book will help many others to take this approach. Since PACTeams are a relatively new concept, we recommend this book as an aid to building one!

1

Hands Free

Ruthie Gilbert

Muddy underfoot with baskets of discarded fruit strewn all over the place, Priscilla and I are threading our way through Ooty market, the early morning mists nipping our noses- 8,000 ft up in the Niligiri hills of South India. Rainbows glimmer in the early light from saris piled on covered wooden tables, scarlet and cerise, sugar-pink and sun-rise yellow vying with shirts of every hue, blue and violet, turquoise, grass green and orange. Adding to the colour burst, the sounds. Shouts, laughter, little children calling, dogs barking, as market traders lay out their wares. We move on into the heart of the market, breathing in spice-filled fragrances and breezes of south-Indian coffee. Contrasts of the centuries - tins of baked beans rubbing shoulders with fans of peacock feathers; old men smoking, and rolling their bedies between gnarled fingers next to betel nut chewing fish-ladies with their big gummy grins stained red, calling for customers.

Through this melee of daily life we are trying to peep through the gaps, to see what we needed to buy on the vegetable stalls. Carrying bags and balancing on tiptoe makes this almost impossible. What we need is hidden from our view behind turbaned broad- shouldered traders, their crisp white dhotis ironed in perfect folds, in brilliant contrast to the riot of activity all around us.

A little tap on my shoulder and I turn to see faithful Ravi, a regular market coolie. 'Any help, today missy?' What a relief. Now it's easy. I thank him, and with a huge broad cane basket balanced on his head and a deftness of speed and strength he follows us, swinging armloads of carrots, cauliflower, broccoli, leeks, sugar, spices, mangos and papayas, coconuts and curry leaves up into his basket, leaving me hands-free and focused on the main task of selecting the best for family and friends.

Later that day Priscilla, her husband John, (two friends visiting from our sending church), Rod and I, were sitting in our home at Hebron School, reflecting together on the next step in our lives. Priscilla said 'You know what you two need? I believe God gave me a picture of it today. A team of basket carriers just like Ravi! Let's work out how we can do that - and we will be two of them!'

For the previous 17 years we had been working in India with Scripture Union. Originally sent from UK we came under the SU India umbrella and fitted very comfortably there. Both of us being 'third culture kids' helped. Rod was born and brought up in India and I in Kenya. Our lives were packed with meaningful cross-cultural activity and along our way we were given some excellent care and encouragement by SU leaders. Friends, both local and foreign, who we call 'God's senior statesmen' arriving at crucial moments in our lives helped too, as we discovered how to exist healthily in the 'Kingdom-building places' God put us in. We lived through deepest sorrows such as the death of our first baby boy at birth in a small Indian town, and also great times of fulfilment seeing the power of God at work in the lives of hundreds of young people in vast schools in India where we worked.

So why did Priscilla suggest that day that we needed a PACTeam - basket carriers - a Personal Accountability and Care Team? And why did it immediately sound so good to

Three reasons.

1. It was the growing awareness of the load of personal care for us as a family that could not be carried by a large mission agency – even with the best of intentions.

2. It was also an alert that we needed a relationship of accountability for us as people, not just for our work with SU. We had a widespread band of prayer-supporting warriors but we could not share intimately with everyone. Our sending church was sending out a growing number of mission partners and had huge involvements locally.

15

3. Perhaps, above all, it was a recognition that we wanted to persevere for the long haul. We wanted to continue to be effective in mission for as long as God intended.

So how does our PACTeam work now?

Perhaps for us, the overriding delight, as well as relief, is that we and these fascinatingly different people are drawn together, connected, by the love of the Father and strong insistent and persistent friendship through all the changing scenes of our lives in mission. This hasn't always been easy, but has been utterly worthwhile. We realise increasingly that God has created us to live in relationship, and 'Kingdom' happens when we lay down our own thoughts, ambitions, dreams and visions and let others speak into our lives and carry the load with us. God rarely is able to use a lone-ranger for long. The effectiveness of our PACTeam has been so radical in our experience that we are convinced that this concept aids God's purposes for anyone wanting to be effective in fulfilling His great commission anywhere, and most particularly for those in cross cultural work.

Following that pivotal picture Priscilla had of basket carriers, beginning with just her and John, gradually the PACTeam has developed and we have identified several baskets or loads that they have been willing to carry for us, to take the burden from us and free us to be effective in our place of service.

Here's a glimpse into a recent gathering while we were visiting the UK:

A knock on the door on a Sunday afternoon

16

*as the PACTeam arrives. Kind and practical
Chrissie bursts in with her arms overflowing
with bulging shopping bags. "Here you are
Ruthie, thought you could do with these.
Sorry it's not more interesting, just useful
stuff." I take a quick peek inside the bags and
see a marvellous variety of juices, cereals,
cheese, fruit and other delicious treats. She's
followed by her husband Andrew, who greets
Rod with a warm bear hug. We have found it
very helpful to have this couple head up our
PACTeam, and through them we funnel a lot
of communication to the rest of the team.
They have visited us in India, Sri Lanka and
Hong Kong. We have breathed the same air,
been bitten by the same mosquitoes, talked
through, walked through, wept through and
laughed through issues together. And soaked
in prayer together. We have been impacted
by their insights. They have kept to the task
of supporting us as a family, with vigour and
passion for the work we are doing without
trying to direct us.*

*Through the sitting room door I catch a
glimpse of Gillian and Brian settling into their
chairs. These faithful friends have been with
us from the beginning, and have, over the
years, carried 'baskets' of finance, volunteer
recruiting, trips to airports, welcome home
meals, prayer walks, and much more. They are
catching up with Betty, who at over 80, still is
a powerful intercessor. And there is Gail, who
almost singlehandedly packed up our little*

house in the UK and unpacked into another within a week of our return, without a single audible groan.

A few minutes later another knock and the rest of the team arrives. Such a wonderful variety of characters we are so honoured to have as friends. Our PACTeam come from several different places. We appreciate the time they take to gather together about once in three months when we are abroad, with extra or specific meetings when we are back in the UK. In between times, they keep in touch with us and each other by email and phone.

After a year away, we are back for a brief three-week family visit. Our time together is limited, and we seem to speak simultaneously, to cover more ground. Andrew, taking the reins of the team, guides us back into a bit of listening to each other.

We don't always agree; in fact we aren't afraid to flesh out our differences of opinion pretty loudly. Gillian is able to draw in the small detail, the nuance, and the insinuations. David, Gail's husband[1], can so often see prophetically the wider picture. Betty finds treasures in hidden places and jots down key points here and there to pass on to her team of intercessors, of which Gail is also very much a part.

We had a wake-up call to what 'money man' Brian

---

[1] Since this book was originally published David, Gail's husband, has sadly passed away. Gail has recently remarried and is still an active member of our PACTeam.

does for us, when he showed us a huge pile of ledgers and notebooks along with computer files which, over many years, he has faithfully kept up to date for us, while also working as a busy accountant. His patience and diligence are second to none. Rod's sister Joy, when able to join us, brings in the strong ties of family and sibling glue. Barbara, bringing her honesty and a smile that lights up the room, only recently joined the team, along with her husband Chris; they add 'spice' as they work in hosting 'Marriage Masala' in the UK, our marriage programme across Asia. John and Serena beautifully blend humour and vibrations of fun with sensitivity to the Spirit's insights. Although seldom able to gather with the team, Serena spent hours editing our first edition of 'Marriage Masala'.

Above all, they emphasise to us how much we need Jesus. We need Him above everything; solid and unflinching. We don't need Jesus for our ministry's sake; we need Him for the pure delight of fellowship with Him. When we lose touch with Him, we lose our peace and joy, can't forgive and get stale. Therefore we need someone to intercede for us. To hear God, to receive His words of wisdom, knowledge and prophecy, backed by Scripture and so draw us closer to Jesus. Recently we were under a lot of pressure, the climate was hot, and we were discouraged. We were starting a new work with a lot of new relationships and a new culture. A buzz on our mobile - an encouraging text had arrived just at the right moment when I was feeling pretty dejected, nursing some stepped-on toes and rather enjoying a self-pitying moan to Rod - 'Hang in there, failure is not an option with Jesus. We are praying'.

19

We want our PACTeam to feel, taste, touch and smell our lives by us being honest and transparent. This is the 'lift' which makes the baskets easier for them to carry, and we are reaping loads of benefits – hands free.

2

Defining a PACTeam

Rod Gilbert

What makes a PACTeam unique?

The concept of a Support Team for cross-cultural workers has been out there for decades. The ground-breaking book 'Serving as Senders' by Neal Pirolo was first published in 1969, and it still, after several revisions, transforms the way people look at mission support, just as it did when it first came out. His second book, 'The Re-entry Team' published ten years later, is a similar textbook for mission support. Most Mission Agencies would have some reference to such a Support Team. For example InterServe say this in their handbook:

> "As part of our responsibility to see that
> support care is provided for all Partners .....
> the Fellowship requires each Partner to have

> a Pastoral Support Group in place in their
> sending country." (used by permission)

However, from our personal experience in cross-cultural work for over 35 years, we realise that greater understanding of this concept is needed to be able to continue long term and avoid burnout. In the last two decades or so, we have discovered the incredible value of such a team of people and doubt very much whether we could have continued as long as we have, without them. We call them our PACTeam[2] advisedly, because they have indeed 'contracted' to journey with us in our missions calling.

In Exodus 17 we have the story of Moses and Joshua's defeat of the Amalakites. Joshua is commanded to take his small army out to battle against the Amalakites on the plain, while Moses goes up onto a mountain to pray. So long as Moses' hands are lifted up in prayer, Joshua succeeds in the battle. Whenever Moses' arms droop, so Joshua's army is overcome by the enemy. To prevent continuous defeat, Aaron and Hur come to hold up the drooping hands of Moses on the mountain, and thus effect a thorough victory for Joshua on the plain. This is a beautiful illustration of how an effective PACTeam can back up and support a mission worker on the field, where without them he or she might flag and falter, failing to achieve the victory God intended.

Then in Psalm 81:6, God says 'I removed the burden

---

[2] It is worth noting that our title, 'PACT to Go', is a play on words. We are not just PACKED and ready to go. We have also made a PACT (or serious agreement) with our supporters back home, that they will have our backs in prayer and in the other kinds of support outlined in the book. And, for our part, we will honour their contribution to the work. This is teamwork and partnership and it means so much!

from their shoulders; their hands were set free from the basket.' This too is exactly what our PACTeam does! We explain this in more detail in the next chapter.

The five elements of a PACTeam simply defined are:

1. **Your PACTeam is a group of your friends, selected by YOU** - not by your church or Agency.

2. **Your PACTeam is primarily concerned about YOU** and your wellbeing wherever God sends you, committed as your 'basket-carriers'.

3. **Your PACTeam does not control you or your ministry** but you give them the right to speak into your life with practical, prophetic, prayerful input.

4. **Your PACTeam does not aim to replace your Agency** or supporting churches at home or local church on the field.

5. **Your PACTeam does not replace the need for healthy local team relationships.**

It needs to be said that we are writing this book assuming that you have heard the call of God, have good standing with your church and their endorsement of your plans, have a sound grasp of what the Bible teaches and experience in sharing the gospel in your own language. You will have received cross cultural training, or your agency will provide orientation, and you go in the power of the Spirit!

There are three reasons why we believe this book is needed.

1. We passionately believe that every individual, couple or family in mission **needs** a PACTeam. We also believe that for those who have such a team, it will eventually become one of the major reasons why they can keep going when others without one, may stop. In the last few years we have been privileged to interact closely with hundreds of mission workers from virtually every continent. We are amazed that many do not have a team supporting them. Of those who do, many seem not to realise how crucial it can be in enabling them to serve long term cross culturally. Of the relatively few who speak highly of their Support Team, we have discovered that their team functions much in the way we are writing about in this book!

2. Every Mission Agency is concerned about 'Member Care'. The debate goes on as to how to do it, who should do it, when to do it, how to pay for it, and even why do it? We suggest that a properly functioning PACTeam can give very practical and workable answers to all these questions, and go a long way to solving them.

3. Newer sending countries, like Korea, India, China, Brazil, are facing the same issues with Member Care, but have relatively smaller funds to realistically address them. We believe a PACTeam can cut through this problem and spread the costs of Member Care over a wider network of people.

Agencies and churches in these newer sending countries, often baulk at the 'extra' costs of even basic member care and are therefore tempted to avoid the issues, sometimes labelling them as 'western problems not so important for us'. Often funds for even basic living are limited, so Member Care can be seen as a 'luxury' which cannot be indulged in. However if all such folk had individual PACTeams, the agency costs of Member Care would come down to a reasonable and manageable amount.

A good PACTeam is an easily affordable, highly efficient, and superbly effective method of 'doing' Member Care. Read on for a broader picture!

.

3

PACTeams around the world

as told to Rod & Ruthie

'Our PACTeam is fantastic. We meet with them – just two couples - every Thursday. They live near us in the same city in India, so this makes it easier to get together. We all attend different local churches, but we meet first to pray, as well as share a meal and our lives together. They help us in practical ways, encourage us in our own lives, help to raise finance and when possible come and join us at the marriage and family programmes we run. – We couldn't do this ministry without them.'

J and C (couple) from South India - to North India

'We have been working in mission for three years based, in Hong Kong, but realise that as well as a wide group of friends who pray for us, we need to put this idea of a PACTeam into practice. This seems to be the gap in our support base. We have decided to return to Canada for a year, to be with family, do some work, and most importantly- build a PACTeam, now we know how to do it. We plan to return to China next year as a family (we have three kids who we home school) with some 'basket carriers' in place.'

B and C (family with 3 children) From Canada - to China

'I have a number of guys who have been praying for me in my sending church youth group and are interested in my work in Japan. But I recognise that I now need to structure this better. I want to ask some of them plus other friends as well to become a PACTeam. I am asking them one at a time. I hope to have four in the PACTeam to start with. I realise I must choose to be open with them and that can be quite tough at times. – I have been back in Hong Kong for several weeks now because of the earthquake, and have discussed with Rod how to form an effective PACTeam. I want to put this in place before I return to Japan.'

M (male aged 27) from Hong Kong - to Japan

'I feel passionate about supporting D and M. I am getting a few of their friends together on Friday for a meal, to catch-up on the news and pray in my house. This may develop into a PACTeam for them long term. It's a small start, but I know they need it. They are only away short term at the moment, but I think there's a lot more to come.'

R (female aged 45) on deciding to 'basket carry' for D and M in Pakistan.

'I have a supportive family, a great church from university and my home church is backing me. I want to link all this together with friends from both places to form a PACTeam before I go to China to teach English next year. I am going with a mission agency who are also encouraging me to take the initiative to do this.'

A (female aged 24) from UK - to China

4

Vulnerability

Ruthie Gilbert

Are you willing to be vulnerable?

The sun was shining, bees were buzzing, the pollen count was 90% and our eyes were streaming, but not just from hay fever. A fortnight earlier we had the devastating experience of being forced to leave Sri Lanka, a country and a work that we loved. The fax read:

> 'You are informed that due to security reasons
> you must leave the country within ten days'.

What followed next was a series of incredible days getting our home of 30 years in South Asia packed into many cardboard boxes and manoeuvring our lives

31

through a tangle of legal wrangling and life-threatening situations, aided by wonderful Sri Lankan friends. So there we were two weeks later in the garden of our house in the UK surrounded by our PACTeam who sat quietly with us as we wept. Their gentle probing gave us a choice, either to be starkly honest and vulnerable, sharing the tears and grief and hopes, or covering up our real emotions by easy, 'I am fine' clichés. I remember consciously deciding to be vulnerable. And I distinctly remember the long, strong, silent hug given by one of the team to both of us, when words were inadequate to express their empathy. It was not all tears. They had arrived with arm-loads of cheeses and flowers and even a bottle of vintage wine to celebrate hope anticipated and an expectation that God, even in this, was going to come through for us again.

Honesty

Why is it that we often find it so hard to be vulnerable? It goes right back to the fall with Adam and Eve trying to live independently from their Maker. In so doing they lost their relationships, instantly became naked and ashamed and had to put the fig leaves firmly in place. Their vulnerability was lost, and with it their ability to trust each other and have an open and honest relationship.

Have you heard of the story of two twelve-year old boys walking round an art gallery? They came across a picture of Eve, a rather glamorous version, with fig leaves placed in the appropriate places. One of the boys walked on, and realising his friend had been left behind, came back and asked 'What are you waiting for?' 'For autumn!' he said, grinning.

Maybe we wait until we get totally to the end of ourselves - when we feel dried out like autumn leaves, physically and spiritually - before we allow people to see us as we are. Or perhaps we wait for other people to be honest, to be real, while we remain comfortable in covering up. Those of us in mission leadership may be particularly prone to that because of a false sense of needing to be perfect – is that not pride? The point is that by covering ourselves with 'fig leaves' we can far too easily trade trust, love, honesty and true friendship with others who are wanting to support us, for alienation, unreality or dishonesty. Is it a risk to be vulnerable? Yes. Is it worth it? A hundred times YES. We will be looking later at choosing the right people to trust to 'hold the baskets' safely.

Being real

We must keep returning to the One who makes life work. As we obey Jesus' instruction to 'seek first the Kingdom of God' we see that the things of life are added to us (Matt 6:33). A vital part of that addition is given to us when we invite a group of people to get close enough to us to see us as we really are. And then allow them to bring strength, trust, care, correction, encouragement and a host of other very necessary things into the mix of the everyday stuff of our lives in cross-cultural work. This will bring us to the end of our attempt to provide all things for ourselves, something our Father has never intended us to do. There may also be times when we feel tempted to focus on past failures and just give up or burn out. If we simply bolt down the

33

hatches of our mind and internalise these things on our own, we can resist God's miraculously free forgiveness. Our own PACTeam friends have been able to say in times of discouragement, sin or failure – 'Who are you Rod, Ruthie? You are a Son and Daughter of the King, a person God loves to be seen with, clean and forgiven. That is your identity'.

What about the pedestals, that other people put us on in times of obvious success? It is so tempting to want to stay on them – you get a grand view from the top. Again, the responsibility is ours, to share our needs and struggles, as well as our victories and successes. This does not mean that we wash our dirty linen in public and shout unwisely across the internet. Instead it means that we willingly deconstruct the myth that a missionary is somehow no longer an ordinary person, but is real with normal human responses, yet one who wants to live in the 'every day miraculous'.

Long-haul wisdom

Ten years before we had to leave Sri Lanka, we were living in India, running a family ministry, with an 'open home' and temperatures rising to 40 degrees plus in the summer. Pressure was building, not only in the mercury but also in the family, with our eldest son returning from university in the UK, three active teenagers, a hyperactive four-year-old and a crazily over-the-top dog. Guests flowed in, through, over and out of our house!

I started to realise something was a bit amiss when I was asked by someone who was browsing through our bookcase, if I was a visitor!

Our ever practical PACTeamers, Gail and David, arrived on the scene. Arranging themselves casually on our low Indian couches, they surveyed this crazy scene for several days. Finally Gail had enough. 'You guys are mad', she said. 'You are never going to survive this. You have got to shut your bedroom door and lock it from the inside, and no one, whose name is not Gilbert should be allowed inside!'

We were living daily in a culture which doesn't generally pay much heed to the need for personal space or privacy, and we simply had been unaware of the toll this was taking on the whole family. We were trying to run a family ministry without any boundaries for our own family life and marriage. We had learned how to have an open door, but not a shut door. It took the wisdom and bluntness of our dear friend to shake us into some reality. A few weeks earlier I had the experience of finding a local friend rummaging through my cupboard, selecting something for herself to wear, so I immediately realised that Gail was talking sense.

We had a choice at that point to listen to Gail or 'cover up' with our greater knowledge of the culture. Had we done the latter we would not have survived for the long haul.

We put her advice into practice. What a relief! As I think back, I can see one of our sons sitting cross-legged in the middle of our double bed, strumming his guitar knowing that he was not going to be accosted by anyone, asked any questions or invited to stand in a photograph for the umpteenth time. We had a place of escape as a family and, in time, another loving friend gave us a gift to air condition that room, to make it not only a refuge but also a cool oasis.

Trust

We had a simple choice at that point to trust that it was God's wisdom coming through Gail's words, and it was His love for us and desire for our very best that was being expressed. Being confronted is never easy, but **from the start we gave our PACTeam the right to speak into our lives, so we knew we had to take notice**. In obedience we acted immediately. Rod jumped on his scooter in the heat of the day to explore the Mahabalipuram market for a little brass bolt, which he expertly fitted to the door.

It may be hard to be vulnerable and yet it is essential. Perhaps the missing element in allowing ourselves to be real and open is basically trust. Indeed one of the key ingredients for a good PACTeam is trust. As we learn to trust our friends and let them carry the baskets for us, it becomes easier to be vulnerable. In truth both trust and vulnerability are also needed for success in any mission venture when we are working with a team. We must honestly recognise that if we find ourselves reluctant to trust and truly be ourselves with other team members it is impossible to develop a true friendship, and an effective working relationship.

Dependence

It is God's role to provide and ours to receive. Independence is simply not an option for us. Therefore the attitude we have to take is not only **for** dependency but also **against** self-sufficiency. We are limited, God is not. We are not self-sustaining, God is. God has planned it so that we cannot live independently but must depend on others if we are going to live 'Kingdom-style'.

Jesus modelled dependency for us all, yet He knew exactly who He was. He was totally aware of what he was called by His Father to do and to be, in other words – he knew His destiny. He also knew he had all the resources of heaven available. If we are to be the same as Jesus in mission, we need to be confident of our destiny and realise we too have the resources of heaven available.

However, this is not a mandate to go it alone. We need people standing with us close enough in relationship to know us as we really are. Jesus constantly demonstrated that He also needed people in this way. He directly asked the Father for His daily bread and told us to do so too (Matt 6:11). But He also asked His closest friends to be present with Him in His darkest hour (Matt 26:38). Jesus stayed connected to His friends, even when they hurt Him or let Him down, and He continued to ask them for help in the Garden of Gethsemane. 'Stay here, keep watch, and keep awake with me'.

This did not mean that Jesus lost autonomy over His life and His decisions, and neither will we. He completed the task the Father had given Him, and so should we. But in His humanity, He needed His friends. If Jesus did, we do - bottom line!

Jesus taught us to pray, 'Your will be done on earth as it is in heaven'. Filled with His presence, the whole atmosphere of heaven is rich in relationships, friendship, love and acceptance with absolute trust. We need to choose daily to do His will and live in that atmosphere of heaven right here, on earth, right now. Only then can we allow ourselves to be vulnerable enough to receive from our friends, be they members of the PACTeam or our fellow missionaries.

5

Creating your PACTeam

Ruthie Gilbert

'I get it.' said Brad, as we were explaining the value of creating a PACTeam to him one warm summer evening. He was working in a school for young drug offenders. Brad with his vibrant wife Crystal, who home-schooled their three young children, was living on one of the outlying islands in Hong Kong.

'Crystal and I have many friends who pray for us and encourage us in Canada and Hong Kong,' he reflected. 'But we have always backed off from asking anything of them because they are so busy. When we try to think of the right people to give us practical support, we hit a brick wall in our minds, so we haven't done anything about getting a specific team together, although we know we need to.'

A lot of mission partners would echo Brad's honest

sentiments, and that is why we want to be extremely practical now in the 'how to' of asking the right people to join your team. We all have different personalities and needs, therefore the format of a PACTeam may vary, but their common purpose will be as 'basket carriers' for you. We will look later at the specific 'baskets' you will need them to carry.

1. Choose S.A.F.E. Friends

PACTeams , as we have said, are made up primarily of your own friends. There may be just three or four friends you could ask or as many as twelve. They may be older, faithful prayer warriors who have known you for years, or new friends you have recently met. They may come from your town or city and just one local church, or a number of places. The common element here is that they are your friends. Some loud and witty, others shy, some quiet, discerning, some highly intelligent, others widely read; some may be artistic, others bringing a keen sense of humour; some who are peacemakers; some extremely practical, some who rock the boat because they are not 'yes' men but willing to look, with you, at the tough stuff of life. They should all be thoughtful, prayerful, attentive friends, with whom you can relax and be yourself. People you love to be with and who make you feel SAFE.

A **SAFE** friend is one who is:

Secure in God themselves and wanting to grow in their love for Jesus

Active - passionate, determined and hardworking.

Faithful for the long haul and willing to take a risk with you.

Encouraging you to persevere!

Consider too this definition of a friend, which focuses on the key ingredients needed in a PACTeam member:- *'A trusted confidant to whom I am mutually drawn as a companion and an ally, whose love for me is not dependent on my performance, and whose influence draws me closer to God'* (J. White).

Bearing all this in mind also remember the five elements of a PACTeam:

1. Your PACTeam **is a group of your friends, selected by YOU**. – Not by your church or agency.

2. Your PACTeam **is primarily concerned about YOU** and your wellbeing wherever God sends you, committed as your 'basket-carriers'.

3. Your PACTeam **does not control you or your ministry** but you give them the right to speak into your life with practical, prophetic, prayerful input.

4. Your PACTeam **does not aim to replace** your agency or supporting churches at home or local church on the field.

5. Your PACTeam **does not replace the need for healthy local team** relationships.

So one of the first things to do when choosing a team is to pray for specific names, and draw up a list of these people while allowing the Holy Spirit to surprise you with His fresh ideas. Perhaps you will *see* faces, situations and needs in your mind's eye. God is always ready and waiting to show us specifics. He knows the plans He has for other people's lives and how they link with our own. God's Spirit wants to teach us how to 'brood over' a matter as He did at creation (Genesis 1:1). We can then pray from His heart and agree with his plans.

If we don't take time to listen to His surprises, we always find we hit a brick wall in trying to get a team together. In fact God may want a very varied group of your friends to really support you and bless your life. We need to listen to His voice and heed the nudges of the Holy Spirit.

Surprised!

Out of breath, looking for a few seats together, we squeezed our way into a space half way up the hall. Why are we always in a rush to make it on time on a Sunday morning? The worship had begun. 'It's all about you, Jesus...um' my mind began to wander, and suddenly, completely out of the blue, I sensed God saying to me –

'Here's your answer, right beside you, ask Chris and Barbara to join your PACTeam'.

A big surprise, as, although we had met them regularly, we didn't know them well. Barbara is Dutch, a warm, friendly midwife and her husband Chris is a finance manager. Barbara had been involved with mission in Africa, where they had met. They had been in the UK since they married and now had three vivacious children.

I tried to focus back into the action as we were worshipping but as a 'do it now' kind of person, I was itching to nudge Barbara there and then and say –

'Hi would you like to be on our supporting team – our PACTeam?'

2. Identify your 'baskets'

We had a need for a friend or friends to join our PACTeam and carry 'the basket' of practical help for our Marriage Masala programme in the UK, and it was this that came to mind when the Lord gave me that 'nudge'. All of us have different needs, but we have identified seven common 'baskets' which you may also want to find a friend to carry. Of course it may be that one person may be willing to lift several off your shoulders.

a. Prayer warrior - Prayer and Intercession

You are looking here for a person or two who loves to pray; a friend who may have a specific gift of intercession, who gives time to listening to Jesus and whom you deeply respect and trust. Expect such a person to contact you with things the Lord is revealing to them and to chase you for answers to prayer or more fuel for prayer.

b. Practical helps

You need here a crucial member of the PACTeam, who is willing to literally get their hands dirty because they love you; someone who takes initiative and motivates others to help as well. It may be as practical as finding a car for you to borrow or arranging to send on your post.

c. Provision - Fund raising and finance

Here you are looking for a friend who has diligence and is able to do some research and a bit of book-keeping. They don't need to be an accountant! An efficient person with a gift for administration would be an asset, along with being someone who is a bit of a 'do it now' person. Procrastination on financial matters is very stressful. Look for someone in whom you can confide your personal needs and financial matters and, of course, who has total trustworthiness.

d. 'Pointman' - A person or couple

This would be someone who co-ordinates your team, and may be able to visit you in your location of mission. An individual or a couple with insight, who will keep to the task of supporting you with vigour and passion for the work you are doing without trying to direct. They will be able to build a strong sense of connection with the rest of your team. You will need to give them the contact details of your team, and they will arrange regular get-togethers whether you are present or away.

e. PR - Personal Relationships

Vital to keep communication rolling; to some extent this involves everyone, but you will probably find that one or two on the team are especially good at keeping in touch with you. Remember to ask someone specifically to send out your prayer letter by email and hard copy.

This takes a huge load off you and keeps you on track with sending out news to your wider supporters and churches. Also this is a 'safety net' as it gives a filter both for unwise comments and spelling mistakes!

f. Particular projects

Such friends may come offering all kinds of specific help. Here are some suggestions:

- web-site designing
- interviewing short-term team members for a mission trip.
- video or short film editing
- giving medical advice - we have had two doctors on our team!

There are more ideas in the check list in appendix A at the end of this book.

g. Planner (or prophet!)

You are looking for a friend who loves the big picture. Who sees the sweep of the horizon before they see the tiny details on a nearby tree! Giving you ideas and suggestions without bias or control - but able to see the wider picture of God's plans for His Kingdom-building worldwide.

As you choose your PACTeam, you may not yet know these people very well. Perhaps one or two have offered to help. You may need to begin small and add gradually to the team. Pray for the inspiration of the Holy Spirit, and be willing to invest massively yourself in building rich and deep friendships over time. Be confident in selecting a team, as you look for the S.A.F.E. qualities.

3. Ask

We have been constantly amazed at how God brings together our ideas of whom to invite to join our PACTeam, with His, to bring about wonderful blessing. He is not against us. He is for us. He likes our friends. He loves them, and has wonderful plans for their lives as well as ours. He has called them as well as us into Kingdom building.

The best time to invite people to form a PACTeam, or to add to a team, is when you are with people in person. It is possible to ask over Skype on a face to face call, but often it helps to have time together to kick off your shoes and settle down to be able to toss ideas, thoughts and possibilities around together.

Their answer was 'Yes!'

That Sunday morning as Barbara was gathering up her family at the end of the service, I asked her, 'Barbara. Would you and Chris be free to meet Rod and me sometime? Could we have a coffee together?'

I felt this was one of Father's surprise ideas for our team, but I wanted to pray it over with Rod and realised that it wouldn't be a good plan to drop the bomb shell of a big request on them there and then.

We fixed a time for later that week. We began by explaining about our PACTeam and the need we had for another couple to be involved in practical help. To our delight, just over the previous few weeks they had been praying that God would show them something new in His Kingdom building that He wanted them to be involved with. Their answer was 'Yes!'

God always wants us to be on target with the right people. He has provision and people prepared. This is always exciting. This also stops us from being self-focused when we choose a team, because God has a huge agenda to bless and extend their borders; not just ours, but theirs too.

Perhaps a major reason that we don't ask people for help is we know that everyone is so busy and involved with their own work and families – how can they think about caring for us too? Right! – and wrong! In China recently we were given an interesting acrostic for being over-busy. *BUSY* = **B**eing **U**nder **S**atan's **Y**oke. Life is full and we are all busy - wherever we are in the world. However by not asking people to help us we are in danger of robbing them of the blessing of being part of His mission call. Ever thought of it that way?

It's true that you rarely consider the requests of good friends an imposition on your time, but we must be prepared not to get offended if they can't immediately respond to our invitation. The key point here is they need to be ASKED. When you ask a friend to join your PACTeam it is helpful to ask the right question - It is not advisable to approach a person by saying 'I know you are terribly busy but....'

Be positive! This is a thrilling invitation! You are asking them first and foremost to join you in living LIFE – wherever God may take you, whatever that may mean, into whatever country or ministry, recognising that may change over the years.

If you are married, the intimacy that is between you as a husband and wife should never be superseded by anyone, but together you are asking this friend to join your PACTeam and be a friend 'that sticks closer than a brother'.

4. How to proceed

Several people have asked us specifically for help in the 'how to' of asking so here are a few samples of invitational questions which may be useful to get you started:

- Would you consider joining our /my PACTeam? Can I tell you more about what I mean?

- I appreciate your friendship. Could I ask for your specific help with my survival in cross-cultural work?

- Would you think about using your gift in intercession as a member of my PACTeam?

- You are a person I really trust. I would like to invite you onto my accountability and care team. How does that sound to you?

- You have encouraged me a lot in my decision to go to .... May I ask you to take up a practical role on my personal accountability and care team when I leave?

- Would you be able to meet at 8 pm next Monday night with a few friends so I can run past you some ideas we have for building a personal accountability and care team before we leave?

- I would really appreciate help with sorting out finances. Would you do that for us as part of our PACTeam? Could we meet and talk more about what this would involve?

- I have noticed how wisely you keep the focus on the key issues in any meeting. Would you be willing to head up our PACTeam? Can I tell you more?

5. Gathering your PACTeam.

Once a few friends have accepted your invitation, quickly arrange a date when you can all meet together. This often takes a bit of juggling and plenty of flexibility on your part.

- Arrange to meet over a meal or light refreshments in someone's home. Remember that they may not know one another; the common element is YOU, as well as the love your share for Jesus and His mission.

- Begin with plenty of time for them to introduce themselves to one another, and say how they met you. Take time to explain clearly your vision, mission responsibility and plans.

- Answer as many questions as you can. Tell them how grateful you are and how you need their help. Be real and vulnerable with your concerns and needs as well as hopes and dreams.

- Run briefly through your expectations for a PACTeam – (explain the 5 elements of a PACTeam mentioned earlier in the chapter.)

- Explain what specific 'baskets' need to be carried for you, and also invite all their ideas as to how they can do this, ensuring that no-one takes too heavy a load.

- At this first gathering, pass on the responsibility of leadership of the team to the Point-person. You probably will already have asked someone, or a couple to do that beforehand. Now trust your PACTeam to get on with the job!

6. Celebrate!

As well as carrying the baskets for you and sharing your burdens, your PACTeam will also be celebrators. They will rejoice in the testimonies of what God is doing through you in the world. It will encourage and build them up, so blessing works both ways.

No matter how involved and busy you get with your work, keep communicating and more communicating!

Jesus must have enjoyed laughing and eating and drinking with His friends. Jews love celebration – I know that from my Jewish father! Imagine the laughter, excitement, dancing and celebration that went on when people got healed; the whoops of delight when bread and fish multiplied.

When you get the opportunity to meet with your

PACTeam friends, as well as discussing and sharing your needs in mission and your ministry, take time to enjoy life together. God has given us all things richly to enjoy and that includes time with our friends!

7. And finally

There are two underlying elements that are essential in creating a healthy PACTeam.

- *Firstly,* you can never thank your team too often, so keep reflecting on how much they are helping you – begin with thanks and continue with thanks. Write cards, send texts, email them, communicate your appreciation fully and freely, not allowing your team to feel that they are being taken for granted.

- *Secondly,* stay aware of how grace covers all relationships. Misunderstandings will arise from time to time as we work in any close relationship. We are all very human – but forgiveness and grace envelop us all. Initiate restoration if you sense that you have offended a team member. Restoration is always easiest while the offense is still recent so keep short accounts with your PACTeamers. Be the first to say sorry.

Hebrews 12:14-15 teaches how determined we must be to 'make every effort to live at peace with all men and to be holy. Without holiness no-one will see the Lord. See to it that no-one misses the grace of God and that no bitter root grows up to cause trouble'.

Your PACTeam will be a place where grace can flow, and forgiveness becomes a lifestyle. It will become a natural part of their encouragement of you to keep you covered by grace for healthy relationships where you are working as well.

At one point we wrote to our PACTeam asking them to pray about an important letter we had sent to a friend to seek to restore relationship.

An email from Barbara came into our inbox the next morning - she was in the UK and we were in Hong Kong – it read simply,

Dear Rod and Ruthie, Will do!
Grace will abound! B.

6

A PACTeam Point Person Interviewed

with Dr Andrew Hill

Andrew, you and Chrissy have been 'basket carrying' for Rod and Ruthie for many years now, can you tell us why you began doing this?

Andrew: Friendship and Relationship! We have known Rod and Ruthie for many years. Chrissy was at school with Ruthie, and the friendship extended and grew first between husbands and then children. They are important to us and we love them. Relationship is more important than anything we can do or skills we may or may not have. Who we are is so much more important in the Kingdom than what we do. Relationship is the basis of any support team.

You and Chrissy are the point-men of their PACTeam how do you feel about this?

Andrew: We are privileged to be part of a team with Rod and Ruthie. It is like playing in a football team with great strikers, but strikers cannot win a game on their own, they need support and a good defence. So we have our part to play as well, part of the team, not just spectators. We rejoice in their victories and share in their struggles. We have a place in defence, praying and listening for them, sharing our thoughts and anxieties from time to time, and freeing them to run, taking care of some of the details that might bog them down a little. We can support, pray, let them know we care and are on their side, and sometimes just be there for them. Team is the right name.

Do you share the vision for their work?

Andrew: God has put on our hearts some of the same desires and hopes that He has for Rod and Ruthie. We care about nations, peoples who have not yet heard the gospel and marriage and family life. We are so grateful for our own family, and want others to enjoy all that God has for us in families. It is easy for us to join wholeheartedly with Rod and Ruthie in their dreams, aims and vision; to be of one heart and mind. We do not want to direct their work; we just want to share in their vision and 'basket-carry' in every practical way possible. Primarily we want to support them as people, as our friends.

What characteristic would you give as a key asset for 'basket-carriers'?

Andrew: Adaptability! I don't think we would see ourselves as being particularly skilled in any of the tasks we undertake, but we will give them a go. We are willing to learn what God can do with us, rather than what we can do for God. That means that we are not stuck in our own perception of ourselves, and can enjoy His enabling and resources. Being willing to give it a go is what is important.

What advice would you give to a global worker creating a PACTeam?

Andrew: Communicate your needs! Rod and Ruthie communicate well with us. They let us know, not just what is happening in their work, but also their family news, their concerns, fears or pain, joys, hopes and vision, and importantly, what parts we can play. They communicate by email, phone, texts (via WhatsApp currently), as well as regular updates and newsletters. We meet when they are here in the UK, individually and as a group. Chrissy and I have visited them in many of the places they have served. As in all teams, good communication is essential. **Communicate well and often**.

7

The PACTeam and your Sending Church

Rod Gilbert

The Biblical precedent of the Sending Church
(See also Appendix B)

We see in the book of Acts a consistent picture of the local church as a place of nurturing and equipping of believers, and also the hub from which all global missionaries were sent out. After all, Paul not only went out from and came back to his sending church in Antioch, but also made sure that new converts were nurtured in churches that he planted. He called them 'partners in the gospel' as he continued his own cross-cultural work across the Roman world of his day. The best preparation for any cross-cultural mission work is to be active in your local church first, finding a place of service and making a good contribution there. That way you will be known for who you are and what you are good at. Your leaders will be able to provide a good reference for your agency or overseas position, because you are known and appreciated where you are. Hopefully the leaders will still be willing to let you go, and will not be like one senior pastor who, when one of his best leaders went forward to respond to a missions call, bluntly said, 'You can't go'. It has to be a good thing if the church would miss the person who goes! It means there is an element of sacrifice involved, and it also means that the support given and interest taken will be strong. If a local church has a vision to engage with reaching the nations, then it is an ideal place for people in mission to receive the support they need as they embark on their journey. It is hugely encouraging to receive the affirmation of the church leaders and their endorsement of the call to go. Receiving their approval also paves the way for the building of a PACTeam, where perhaps the core members will be active in that church as well. Possibly the church leaders have experience of what to look for in an agency, or even have existing relationships with good agencies, so can help on that count too, and also with re-entry or returning.

A different perspective from the PACTeam

Having understood this, we need to recognise, however, that the sending church has a different perspective from the PACTeam. The focus of the PACTeam is specifically for the individual or the family that is sent out, while the church is focusing on its whole body of people. A local church mission secretary or mission board may be appointed to ensure that finance is raised, the church is motivated to pray, and information is properly disseminated within the church. This will ensure that Mission is kept high on the agenda of the church. There may be several global workers sent from your church and it will probably not have sufficient resources to ensure that each one receives adequate pastoral care or maintains satisfactory personal accountability.

Why is a PACTeam needed in addition to a sending church?

All of us differ, and equally our situations will vary. We can only draw out some general observations, which may or may not apply to you. Remember, though, that we are in no way seeking to diminish the importance of your sending church.

1. In the long term the local church in the country and place of mission becomes the home church. The closer you, as a person in mission, identify with the host culture, the more distant the ties may become back home. Mission agencies encourage this level of identification, particularly those from the newer sending countries, and cross-cultural workers may become so integrated in their new cultural home that they slowly lose their identity as a foreigner. Ties with the original Sending Church may therefore change in nature. Your PACTeam, on the other hand, is friendship based and so, whatever happens, it will continue to function and keep in touch with you and visit you, as your friends.

2. Home churches can also radically change over the years. New leadership can come in and alter the direction of the church or attitude to mission work positively or negatively. Sometimes this can lead to members leaving, or a church plant being set up, or even a church split. This can be hugely distressing for you, wherever you are across the world, and often causes conflicting loyalties for you, wondering where your home-base now is. You then have to find ways of retaining the good ties you had previously, as well ways of forging new ties that will last. A PACTeam is immensely valuable in doing this with you, and continuing to carry the baskets for you no matter what is happening.

3. The third practical issue not easily addressed by the sending church is when the mission family is from two or more countries. Over many years of debriefing mission families, while working in Hong Kong and now in the UK at Kings Mill, we have encountered many cross-cultural marriages. Indeed our own five children are all in cross-cultural marriages! With such families, home church support is complicated to say the least. Only a very few have organised support in both countries. Most have concentrated on just one of the countries. Others fall between both and struggle hard to keep good connection. All such cross-cultural families can benefit hugely from a PACTeam, which

can help bridge this gap – being drawn
from the strengths of networks of friends
and churches in both home countries.
Contact, now so simple over the internet,
makes a transglobal PACTeam, or even two
separate PACTeams, a very viable option.

A PACTeam helps with giving strong and continuous support

There need be no confusion of roles as between a PACTeam and a sending church. If PACTeam members are also on the Mission board of your sending church that may be a benefit. However, particularly in matters of finance, they may need to remain objective in decisions the church may have to make. Some mission partners may not find it easy to keep communication flowing, or may feel unsure about how to pass on information, fearing it may affect their financial support. This too can be covered by your PACTeam who will keep the sending church up to date with news and needs, so that the sending church continues to be kept well in the loop.

You may have more than one sending church. The PACTeam will be particularly effective if you draw on friendships from the different churches and you will feel a sense of unity as the PACTeam holds together the wider body of Christ in supporting you. You might find you have been assigned to a house group that will need encouraging with regular updates. Your PACTeam will be able to maintain good links with them and you will be encouraged by their faithful prayer. It may be that you are the only one sent from your home sending church. You may have grown spiritually in that church, so you have trusted friends functioning like a PACTeam with whom you allow yourself to be vulnerable, and with whom you have made a commitment of mutual accountability. You may see an overlap between the role of the sending church and this book's recommendation for a PACTeam. You would do well to acknowledge this and formalise relationships into a PACTeam. By specifically telling these close friends that you see them as your PACTeam, you will encourage them and ensure that personal accountability and care will continue, even if those friends move to other places. A PACTeam made up of your friends will not be susceptible to the inevitable changes that happen in local church life and can, uninterrupted, give that strong and continuous personal support. This therefore assists the role of the sending church(es) to enable you to continue on in the call God has put on your life, as an expression of the work of His Church worldwide.

The Joy of Synergy

What a joy it is to come across some local churches that see their mandate as being missional both at home and 'to the ends of the earth'. They want to equip all their people for reaching out and are willing to send their best to the nations, as God directs. For such churches we simply to offer the concept of PACTeams as an add-on benefit to what they are already doing by way of support – a means of making their job of supporting those they send out as effective as it can be for the long haul. We want to encourage pastors to see a PACTeam as *complementing* what they are already doing by way of support, not in any sense in competition.

8

Back Pack to PACTeam

Maria Raftery

Preparation

As a basket-carrier in my sister's PACTeam I would like to tell the story of how this has worked for her so successfully over the years.

My sister V is 5 years younger than me, and when she was born, I was trusted to hold her and feed her, so I took on the 'big sister' role, literally carrying her at a very early age. When she was in her early 20s, she followed the hippy trail overland to Kathmandu as a single woman in survival mode, with a back pack and no thought for anyone but herself. Along the way she found salvation. A few years later, when she responded to the call to serve long term overseas, she got financial and prayer support from her home church, joined a global mission agency with links with her chosen destination and travelled round the UK raising support. This time she left, still with a back pack, but also with complete faith that God would provide everything she needed for the long haul, although at the time she didn't realise how much 'basket carrying' she would need!

Provision

That was back in 1994. I don't remember the details except that the Agency required her to have a bank account with them and I was to reimburse her expenditure countersigned by the mission secretary from her home church. It soon became apparent from my experience in international banking that this would not work in the country where V had gone. I had to persuade the finance director to let her use a credit card as her only means of getting local currency. I then paid for everything else from the UK bank account, so V never really knew how much money she had available.

Some things have become easier for us over the years. It was wonderful to be able to communicate by email instead of letters taking 3 weeks. Before V visits the UK there are medicals and hospital appointments to be arranged, hire car to be booked and I also liaise with people over her speaking itinerary. Some areas have become more complicated. We bought a house for her retirement with a mortgage from the Agency and I rent it out.

I have power of Attorney and the abundant grace of God!

Prayer

V sends home the most amazing hand written prayer letters with news and photos, praise and prayer points. No self adhesive envelopes and stamps when we first started so I adopted a banking technique of using a wet sponge on the gum, to spare my tongue, as I regularly mailed out something like 170 letters and acknowledged each response. We still send the prayer letters by post and people still love receiving them that way and continue to respond generously in prayer and provision. I also get calls regularly for updates before church prayer meetings.

Personal Relationships

It was with great joy and some trepidation the first time I visited V loaded down with so many necessities for her, made in that country but for export only. I also took her insulin (V has had type 1 diabetes since she was 10), replacement credit card (unsigned, before the days of chip & pin), and a few thousand pounds in blank travellers cheques (the only means of getting a substantial amount of money into the country for her to pay language college fees). I felt nervous, like a smuggler, as I waited in the crowd to pass through Arrivals until my walkman (which now would be an iPod), played 'Enter his gates with thanksgiving in your heart, enter his courts with praise'.

My visits have been a brilliant time of hiking, praying, praising, assessing and FUN. Once we went up to 14,000ft (4000m) and were breathless at God's beautiful and awesome creation (we declined to buy bottled oxygen!). We got to places 'tourists' would not have been allowed. Visits have also been the opportunity to sort out practical issues. On one occasion I was able to negotiate improved housing facilities with her field leader so she could install a solar panel for hot showers!

Over the years I have been able to build up relationships with others supporting V and I remember one trip when I spent 5 days on a river boat writing 200 postcards from us both.

PACTeam building

Purposefully 'carrying the baskets' for V has been straightforward because we have a strong relationship as sisters. It has been easier for me to take on a number of roles, but the principle of needing a PACTeam applies, and I can hand the baskets over to others to carry.

V is very good at letting her whole PACTeam know what help she needs, and ensures I don't get overloaded. When V comes back to the UK she spends the time visiting the many churches and individuals, who support her financially and in prayer, to share the word of God and to update them on the work of God.

I am aware V has a number of special relationships with church leaders to whom she holds herself personally accountable. One time, before she moved on to a new area, her home church leader came out to commission the local leaders of 3 churches that had been established. She is in regular contact with the field director and also has visits from the UK Missions director. The PACTeam plays a very important role in supporting her as a *person* while her Agency carries the responsibility for the *work*.

As I checked the facts, I realised that 1994, the year V completed her theology degree and went to work overseas, was also the year I gave up a 'high flying' banking career because my daughter was born with special needs. I am sure when God calls someone into missions, he also calls others prepared to play a supporting role. Whom he calls he equips, so make it a priority to track down the people you need to develop a PACTeam so you can be blessed and encouraged to stay the course as each one does their bit to fulfil God's plan and purpose.

9

Perfect PACTeam

Alastair and Rosalyn Reid

We are teachers from the UK, and would like to share our story of nine years in India by the amazing grace of God and the loving kindness of our friends.

I, Alastair, was given the post of Principal Designate and Rosalyn that of a teacher at this 100 year old co-educational boarding school for Christian workers' children.

'I was petrified', says Rosalyn 'but we were both convinced it was right, when we were appointed to Hebron School in South India in 2000. With our own three children, then aged 16, 14 and 12 years of age, this was a major move for us all and not one we undertook lightly or on our own!

Inspired by the book *'Serving as senders'* by Neal Pirolo, in which he suggests that for one person to go nine people are needed to help at home, we were able to gather a group of friends from our home church, and from Dean Close School in Cheltenham, where Alastair had been Deputy Head for 5 years. (Dean Close is an independent day and boarding school which has a clear Christian foundation and has supported many missionary families over the years.)

The PACTeam

We were sent off by 12 wonderful people, including an accountant, willing to take on various supporting roles. Amazingly over the years, as someone had to step down, another immediately replaced them. The team was later joined by a couple who had also served at Hebron and another who came on a school inspection. It was so helpful to have those with valuable insight into our current situation. The PACTeam met every 6 weeks or so to pray for the family, monitor our financial support, and organise any practical help.

Prayer

We are so grateful to Diane and Andrew Bruckland who regularly hosted prayer meetings for us. We knew we could, and indeed must, be honest with the PACTeam as they were committed to us, so we did not need to feed them an edited version of the challenges of life in India. We were able to email urgent requests at any time and know they would be passed on to the faithful, prayer warriors who were supporting us.

70

We are also thankful that the PACTeam maintained the data base and sent out our prayer letters by email and 'snail mail' playing an important part in keeping us in touch with all those supporting us by prayer and giving financially.

Provision

In August 2000, we set out in faith with only a small salary from Hebron School, the monthly giving of a few of our friends and the determination to manage on that! A real blessing was the advice from another friend who had served in India for many years: 'Buy and rent out a one-bedroom bungalow in the UK!' Our accountant friend managed the finances with Power of Attorney which was a huge weight off our shoulders. We were offered free storage space for our personal belongings and as we ended up being away for 10 years, it saved us a fortune.

As we look back, we see how the PACTeam played such a vital role, including organising and helping to fund our eldest daughter's wedding in 2005. We were overwhelmed with so many instances of generosity.

Also in 2005 we had to decide whether to return permanently to the UK in 2006 as planned, or take a sabbatical for 6 months before returning for a final 3 year contract until 2009. This was such a crucial decision that we came back to the UK to see the PACTeam to discuss and pray through face to face as we always valued their wise and considered advice. The PACTeam provided a flat rent free, and it was such a comfort to have a home base, our own front door, and room to have our adult children stay. They also sorted out a car for us to use.

Then, when we returned to India for a final 3-year contract in 2006, one of the PACTeam contacted all our supporters to increase their giving. This meant when we returned to the UK, we were able to set up home again with money behind us to help with so many necessary expenses.

Presents and Presence

We were so touched by the PACTeam remembering our birthdays and sending us all presents at Christmas. They kept us up to date with precious news from home and sent 'goodies' unobtainable in India, particularly in the early days when we missed the taste of home.

We loved all the visits from folk who came to see us. It was so much easier to share the joy of serving at Hebron when our friends could see and then report back home the wonderful things God was doing in us and through us at Hebron. One of the PACTeam even came on a teacher exchange for a whole term! We were especially encouraged by the ones who came to help in the medical centre and as part of a school inspection team to help Alastair when he became Principal in 2002.

Parenting

Of course our children grew up and had to leave as they had no visas to stay in India. As they in turn returned to the UK for gap years and university, it was so reassuring to have the PACTeam gently supporting them. They had seen our children growing up in India and had a deeper understanding of the cultural adjustments they had to make as young adults. Owning a house, staying on the electoral roll, and keeping a base in the UK also helped when it came to arranging for UK status for our children as they attended university.

We all found the booklet '*Care Across Cultures*' by Cherilyn Orr very insightful and would recommend it to any church supporting missionaries. (cherilyn@ globalmission.org)

Preparing for re-entry

In the summer of 2008 the PACTeam committed to work through the process of returning us intact to the UK and found Neal Pirolo's book '*The Re-entry team*' very useful. In addition former Hebron staff shared their experience.

We were so grateful for the support and care shown by each one of the faithful friends appointed by God and were able to express that at a thanksgiving service held at our supporting church. We so appreciate the time and energy the PACTeam devoted to us and have often suggested this to other staff at Hebron as we are convinced it was a major factor enabling us to remain so long overseas serving the Lord. They remained committed to us in prayerfully practical ways as we made the transition back into the UK and to a new home in Hampshire.

10

The PACTeam and your Mission Agency

Christine Paterson

"Mission agencies are like people - they have different personalities. Each candidate needs to get to know several agencies, find out how they operate, and ask the Lord where they fit".
(From 'Ask a Missionary' website, which is well worth a visit, on this and other related topics:
http://www.askamissionary.com/topic/
mission-agencies)

Google a simple question like 'what is a missions agency?' and you will be met with a plethora of different answers and a bewildering number of agencies to choose from. But it is harder to find a helpful definition of what a mission agency actually is! Formerly known as 'missionary societies', agencies are organisations that are designed to facilitate the fulfilment of the Great Commission in the foreign countries where they operate, and to provide an umbrella for their members to work there under them. In some cases there may be a particular focus on just one area of the world or even a target people group. Whatever it is, the agency will have a clear mission statement, and it is this vision that normally attracts someone to join its ranks initially. The selection of the right agency is hugely important, because so much rides on the outcome of that choice. As the quotation at the beginning of this chapter suggests, time needs to be taken to carefully consider the nations served by the agency, its doctrinal basis and ethos, the requirements for application, questions about training and the raising for support, amongst other issues, in order to determine how the Lord is leading.

Agencies are such are a late invention from the birth of the modern missionary movement at the end of the 18th century, and much missionary endeavour had taken place over centuries before that without them. We ourselves set out without a mission agency, and we did not intend to form one. However as our work developed, we morphed, we changed, and we grew, and eventually we saw our responsibility to care for the people who had felt an affinity to our values and been drawn in to work with us. We had to learn fast what it takes to be responsible for the people who follow us. As a small company, however, we also needed to keep our focus on what our specific role was.

Ideally an agency provides at least some, if not most, of the following:

- Cross-cultural training, preferably if possible, actually in the host culture. Otherwise this needs to have taken place in some other context beforehand. A proper understanding of the host culture is vital, as well as coming to grips with, and a laying down of, our own cultural pride!

- Orientation to life in the new context and help through culture shock.

- Help through language study, if needed.

- Help in defining the right place of service locally and in obtaining the necessary visas.

- On-field supervision and work accountability.

- A sense of belonging to a bigger whole – enhanced by a prayer network and the mutual care of fellow team members.

- A first port of call in a crisis – emergency procedures should be in place.

- Mentoring in mission life skills – a context for older people in mission to offer their wisdom and experience, while younger people bring their energy, fresh perspective and new talent to the table!

- A regular gathering – a chance to share needs and opportunities and receive spiritual refreshment and renewal of vision and purpose.

Some agencies or companies require a long period of pre-field training, gaining Bible and other qualifications.

But what if, after all that time and costly investment on the part of agency and sending church – not to mention the candidates themselves – the prospective candidate turns out to be unsuited to life on the field? What if they arrive in the new culture all eager and ready to serve, but simply cannot adjust or cope with the challenges? That, in part, is what the new sending countries baulk at; so many wasted resources going through all that training, and then such a disappointment!

In the case of our own organisation, we decided to take some of the 'riskiness' out of this process, by offering a year-long course in cross-cultural training, actually in the country where we worked. Although this no longer exists in that particular form, it has been adopted by a sister agency, and some courses coming out of it are now going online into the 'cloud'[3]. As a stand-alone programme, such a school (which we would run as four months of 'theory' and seven months in some kind of practical service), is, in itself, a beneficial life experience for those who are considering a missions 'career'. Almost everyone who went through ours, over a decade of running them, was grateful for the lessons learned and the measure of in-depth exposure they had to a very different culture from their own. In addition, it gave us, the agency, a chance to observe the student's ability to adapt to our organisation's own internal culture and values, which to us was also part of the purpose. At the end of the year, a mutual assessment would take place as part of the debriefing process, as both parties prayerfully decided if the fit was right for the long term. For those who stayed, this course was the gateway into the organisation, and a year of

---

[3] See www.fieldpartner.org for English

cultural adaptation had already taken place. For those who decided to return home, it had hopefully been a valuable cross-cultural learning experience that they would look back on and treasure. Such people prove, incidentally, to be excellent PACTeam members, as by now they know from the inside what life on the field is like! Mary was one such person, and she gives us a fascinating account from her perspective in Chapter 12.

How does a mission agency's focus differ from that of a PACTeam?

1. While a PACTeam's concern is exclusively for the welfare of the individual, couple or family it supports, an agency has to keep a 'big-picture' focus on its ministry in the part of the world where it serves. Not only is there a history of involvement there, but there is also a vision for continuity into the future and a sense of responsibility for the on-going work. New recruits receive guidance from the agency on how to live and behave appropriately in the culture, while bringing with them a Kingdom Culture that supersedes all our human political and cultural norms and sensitivities.

2. At the same time, of course, an agency must also be committed to the welfare of its members. From "recruitment to retirement" is a slogan used to describe the scope of an organisation's commitment to Member Care. This is people care, but

in a broad sense of making sure that the systems are in place for members' needs to be served on the field. An agency should be ready to give support through all sorts of life events that happen along the way - episodes of culture shock, personal crises of various sorts, conflict resolution or, often forgotten, the stress of re-entry to one's own culture. This cannot, however, be with the same degree of personal involvement as a PACTeam can offer. The PACTeam, by definition, keeps its focus on the detail in your personal life and the toll, perhaps, that living on the field takes on you and on your family.

3. For an agency, this commitment to the person in mission is logically only for the duration of their involvement in the organisation. If the person leaves, for whatever reason, or moves to another country not served by that particular agency, then the long-term commitment ceases. A PACTeam, on the other hand, takes on a commitment to that worker as their friend for the long haul, and 'moves on with them', as it were, should they leave their agency or move to another sphere of service.

Thus the main difference between a mission agency and a PACTeam is that the PACTeam (as the name suggests) primarily functions to provide for the individual's personal accountability and care; while the agency seeks to provide the same in the context of work and of the wider ministry as a whole. Of course there will be overlap, but this distinction is vital for our understanding of a healthy relationship between the two.

Are mission agencies actually needed in the 21st Century?

Having reached this stage in the book, you might well be wondering whether agencies are needed at all, if the PACTeam model of care works so well. Many would argue that they are not – there are missionaries all over the world today, who have gone out with only their sending church behind them. As mentioned before, this was the case for Ross, as far back as 1969 when that was somewhat rare. This **can** be enough, provided there is an effective PACTeam, and provided that the worker is encouraged to network well with others in the locality where they are working. However, it is our belief, through bitter experience of learning things the hard way, that especially in the early days, wherever possible, it is truly advisable to have the support of an agency, as well as of a PACTeam, behind you. Just as you never get a second chance to make a first impression, as the saying goes, so you never get a second opportunity to build a good foundation in cross-cultural work. Having help to adapt well to the culture *at the very start*, is for us an absolute key. Even beyond that, there is a specific niche contribution from the agency, which is very hard for either the sending church or a PACTeam to fulfil. It comes from years of experience and history in that culture, the building of local friendship and knowledge and networking.

81

After a period of time of becoming seasoned in the cultures, some workers, especially those with a pioneering nature, may feel they would work better without the 'branding' of being involved with a certain agency. After a while, though, they may also find that others are drawn in to work with them, so they need to step up in leadership and responsibility to provide care and accountability, and thus a new agency is born!

We don't need to do it all!

There are some tough issues that arise that are way beyond what either PACTeams or most agencies can provide for those they support – debilitating depression, eating disorders and serious marital difficulties, to mention but a few. Sometimes there can be accidents, emergencies or political crises that call for immediate action. Agencies need to have a quick response procedure for such eventualities and know where else they can then refer people for more in-depth help – crisis or trauma debriefing, for example. Worldwide there are now centres for specialist care offering resources wider than any single agency can provide.

For us on the agency side, there comes a great liberation with the realisation that we **don't** have to do it all – in fact we neither can nor should! On the micro-level there is the sending church working with the PACTeam back home, as well as team members and local friends on the field. And on the macro-level, there are these member care centres, with specialists committed to offering a wide range of help. So the agency, functioning in between, needs to keep its own focus on fulfilling the specific mandate the Lord has given for the advancement of His kingdom. If the pastoral needs are well taken care of, then this leaves the overseers on the field free to do the job of leadership, envisioning and mentoring, so that the work can go forward well.

A final thought

Agencies come in many guises and sizes, some with generations of history, some relatively new. There is room for all sorts in the building of God's Kingdom, as we follow the leading of His Spirit. The PACTeam and the sending church take the strain out of pastoral care and the agency supplies what the others can't do on the field. What an exciting synergy we have here!

Rod suggests that the PACTeam concept could provide the answer for the newly emerging sending nations, where the huge cost of Member Care is an issue. We would add, that schools of mission described above, with training on the field while learning to live in that culture, perfectly completes the model

During the course we offer, vital matters are covered such as maintaining personal intimacy with God, understanding spiritual warfare (especially on the 'front line'!), the history of missions and what has been accomplished by others before us, and 'how to read the Bible for all it is worth'. We also include the Kairos Course[4], which imparts an essential understanding of God's heart for the nations. And of course we also give a thorough introduction to the culture we serve.

---

[4] See http://www.kairoscourse.org/index.php/about-kairos)

Last but not least, we include a strong plug for the building of PACTeams, with teaching from Rod and Ruthie! This model, we suggest, fits the mobility of the 21st century, as well as being within the reach of newer sending nations to manage financially.

11

Proactive PACTeam

Lydia's Story

Having been abroad for over three years now, I, Lydia, have become more and more convinced of the absolute necessity of a PACTeam. I can honestly say that I wouldn't have made it this far if it were not for my gang at home and the support they give.

Getting Started

When I was preparing to come out to East Asia it was suggested to me that I should raise up a prayer support group who would meet every month to uplift me as a CCW. I thought that this should probably be a group of folks who were fierce intercessors who had a heart for East Asia. As it turns out, those people are few and far between, so I had to reconsider my criteria! After some thought and prayer, I figured that the people I could rely on most to be faithful in prayer were my closest Christian friends. These guys did not have a heart for East Asia (and were mostly wondering why on earth I wanted to go there!) but they did have a heart for me, and believed in the calling that the Lord has over my life. I know that if I were to uproot tomorrow and move to India or Timbuktu, they would continue to support me wherever God leads. Where initially they were set up as a prayer group, their role has evolved to be so much more for which I am very grateful.

Keep going

After I arrived in East Asia and began to settle in, I realised that being a CCW was not as straight forward and uncomplicated as I had thought it might be. The culture shock of landing in East Asia was one thing, but the surprise for me was the culture shock I experienced within the team there, who comprised of just about every western nationality and all the different flavours that come with them. Despite some great friendships within the team, it's easy to feel a little lost and misunderstood in these very diverse groups with a confused cultural identity. My PACTeam has been a real anchor for me.

Linking up

My PACTeam consists of thirteen people who have committed to pray for me as individuals and also to meet each month to pray together. There is an older couple in their 70's, four couples in their 30's just starting to have children and three single folks. One of the couples always hosts the meetings in their home and two of the women co- lead the meetings and stay in close contact with me each week so they are always on top of what's going on in my life.

I send them (and a lot of other people) my monthly newsletters updating them on the work that I'm doing and how things are going generally, but we have a fair bit of contact in between where they really get involved in the nitty gritty of my life out here. Of course they are interested in the work that I'm doing and are keen to see God's kingdom come in East Asia, but they focus more on supporting me so that I can be the best that I can be to do the work that God has prepared for me. This may involve just letting me talk and process things externally as they offer objective advice or simply lend an understanding ear. It may be that they deal with practical needs that arise, like raising financial support for unexpected expenditures such as replacing a broken laptop or sending out medication etc or more importantly chocolate!

The PACTeam and I are in this together as partners. I know that I can't be a CCW out here without them, and they know it too. My concerns become their concerns and they stand with me through it all. I know I can come to them with anything and trust them with everything. They celebrate with me in the successes and good times and they cry with me in the challenges and the tough times. We have grown together over the last few years and as my love and heart for East Asia has grown, so has theirs. In fact, Mary, who was heading up my PACTeam caught such a passion for the place that she came out and spent last year serving in East Asia alongside me!

12

PACTeam by Skype

Mary's story

I guess my main involvement with all things PACTeam related began 3 years ago, when I, Mary, started leading one (!) for a good friend of mine who became a CCW. I led the team for 2 years, before becoming a CCW and being supported by a team myself! So I have found myself in the slightly unique position of being both the provider and the receiver in the world of missionary support! (I'm fairly sure there's a sporting analogy in there somewhere!).

Getting started

When I was asked by my friend to begin leading this group, I had no previous experience or 'qualifications' for the job, other than being someone who she knew and trusted; someone who cared and wanted to be involved in her adventure. Actually I think for a PACTeam leader this is all that is essential. Being someone who can be available to really share and partner in their life, someone who they would take direction from if needed, and ultimately, someone with whom they feel they could share anything and be assured of the genuine listening heart on the other end. I considered it a huge privilege and honour to be able to stand alongside Lydia. The fact that we were thousands of miles away from each other made no difference!

Keep going

Certainly when I later went into CC work myself, I found it really is the support from back home that keeps you going. It makes a tremendous difference knowing that people who love and care for you are fighting your corner, both in prayer, for practical needs back at home, and just simply by staying involved in your life. It is hard to describe how you cope living in a foreign culture, where nothing is easy and straightforward, and you can find yourself so often misunderstood. Just by having a few people who know you inside out, and who you can totally be yourself with for those few minutes you are in contact, it really is invaluable. Even if it's only to share something relatively small that you know the other person would find interesting or entertaining! In fact regular contact by email/ Skype/phone call/ posting parcels (any or all of the above!) is something that we both agree we could not live without, well that and chocolate of course!

Linking up

When we had our regular group meetings for Lydia, we would have a copy of her latest newsletter with updates and prayer requests etc, but I would try not to make that the priority and sole focus of the group. I felt strongly that we were a bunch of her close friends who cared and wanted to know in detail how she herself was doing, what was going on with her, and situations that were on her mind and heart. I would always make sure I had spoken to her recently, often the night before, to have a catch up and to ask those questions with answers that were not always possible to obtain via a newsletter update. I would then relay to the group anything extra I felt was needed, and we could really seek the Lord for all areas of her life, not just the CC work. And then the next time I spoke with her I could update her with encouragements and anything else that had drawn our attention.

PACTeam working via Skype

Often we would arrange to Skype her during our meeting. This was a great way of just being able to hang out together as friends, and give us all an opportunity to see one another if we hadn't for a while. It also gets everyone in the PACTeam immediately involved in a very tangible way, which is encouraging for them as well.

Speaking now from the point of view of being supported, this was always really important to me, especially if I was struggling. There is something about physically being able to see the people who are gathered and partnering with you that is so comforting. Of course the only trouble with this is the time difference! The UK was 7, and in the winter 8, hours behind us in East Asia, so the general evening meeting slot in the UK calculates to the early hours of the morning for whoever was expecting the friendly call! But, again speaking from my own experience too, we were always more than happy to get up and chat, even if we didn't look like it for the first 10 minutes! I do remember one time when I was leading the group back in England and we had arranged a Skype date, everything was in place, all technical issues (which tend to crop up from time to time!) were sorted, we were just waiting for the signal to say she was online - which never came! - So after a while of waiting patiently we decided to be mean and phone her on her mobile, knowing full well why she wasn't online (after all it was 3am her time!). As expected, the phone was answered with a very sleepy sounding "hello"! Needless to say after 10mins and a quick cup of coffee she was back on form and we had a great chat!!

I cannot stress enough the absolute necessity of the PACTeam. They go on the journey with you - step by step, excitement by excitement, and challenge by challenge – and I really believe that no CCW can survive long term without one!

13

Pitfalls to Avoid

Rod Gilbert

'Aren't you being too idealistic? You happen to have a unique PACTeam. It doesn't work for most people.'

These were the words of very close friends who had been in cross- cultural work for more years than we had. As we listened to them, we realised that we had forgotten some of the mistakes we had made in our very early years in mission. We were assuming too much. This chapter is therefore a brief reminder of some of the pitfalls we, or others, have experienced and you may well come across, if your PACTeam is not set-up correctly or functioning as it should.

1. You cannot assume your PACTeam is the be-all and end-all!

Much as we totally and wholeheartedly support the necessity of a PACTeam, your agency is crucial - and the team of colleagues you will have around you - either physically near, or organisationally near. The immediacy of their presence and the depth of their experience and wisdom are vital. A good cross-cultural worker will have built strong, dependable and trustworthy relationships with his/her colleagues on the field. We recall with so much joy the rich friendship and support we received from our colleagues in Scripture Union, India. We were the only foreign workers with SU India at the time, and we worked under our Indian leaders and our local committee's direction. The annual gatherings of all the staff together, members of almost every state in India, and often in some fascinatingly exotic location, were a special thrill. I remember marching around the courtyard of the centre we were staying in, reciting, as we stamped one foot after the other, 'Train and Trust'. This was the theme of the conference. To all of us it was life forming, as we each went back to our separate places of work all over India, committed to 'Train' our young people in ministry to children and youth, and then 'Trust' them to do the job – seeing them making mistakes, but being at hand to pick them up train again and trust some more - an ever continuing cycle; an attitude of life I have never forgotten in all our cross-cultural work.

As time and language progress, your ability to draw strength from the local fellowship of believers will grow stronger and stronger. In Sri Lanka, for example, we made very deep and lasting relationships with several mature local Christians. In fact, we came to rely heavily on the wise counsel and insight of one dear brother, whose early morning telephone calls during a particularly stressful time, inevitably contained just the right word for us as we faced up to some life-threatening situations in our work. Our PACTeam was a wonderful support also, but that dear brother was used by God to guide us through situations that no other could have. *Remember your PACTeam has its limitations!*

To think through:

- How do I balance my relationship with my PACTeam versus my friends and teammates in my place of cross-cultural work?

- Are there areas of my life I would prefer that only my PACTeam knows about?

2. You must not confuse the role of the sending church with the PACTeam

We have briefly looked at the role of the sending church in Chapter seven. However there may be some delicate areas to navigate, especially where your sending church feels very attached to you. Most sending churches will be only too happy for others to be involved in your support, but you may need to arrange a meeting between your PACTeam and your sending church mission committee or pastor so that there is no misunderstanding. It may also be wise to specify together the areas where one or the other is responsible – that may even need to be formalised in a Memorandum of Understanding. Essentially you need to win the heart of your pastors so that they see your PACTeam as a Good Thing, not something that will write them out of the equation. You need to actively respect your Pastor's leadership, and at the same time keep the freedom to choose your own PACTeam members. We realise that this may not always be easy.

In some unusual cases, your sending church mission committee may BE your PACTeam, and there may be no need to create another one. This is rare though, as the essence of a PACTeam is that its members are YOUR choice, not anybody else's, and specifically your own friends.

To think about:

How can you honour your sending church leaders, as you create your PACTeam?

3. Problems arise if you leave your PACTeam out in the cold

David, after 3 years of concentrated language study is now deeply engrossed in ministry and has been pioneering a new area for his agency. He is excited and hugely fulfilled. Sally, his wife, is similarly involved. Together they are 'on a roll'! Their PACTeam e-mails to ask what issues they need to pray for at their next meeting. David sends them the prayer summary that has gone to all his prayer supporters, and asks them to use their spiritual discernment to know how to pray for him and the family, telling them that he will write later with more details. He doesn't write. There are too many other pressing needs to deal with. Three months later they write again, and David and Sally give them the same response – except that Sally does manage to add a few family health issues that have been concerning her. The PACTeam faithfully meet and pray. They begin to wonder what their role is. "Are we here just to rescue them when they get into problems?" they wonder.

After several months of this kind of response, the PACTeam begins to lose heart, and David and Sally are rather annoyed to find their PACTeam seems distant when they request them to try to find a car for them to use on their next visit home!

The problem clearly is that their PACTeam feels uninformed and unappreciated. Undoubtedly the Agency was quite happy to leave David and Sally to get on with things alone, having quite enough to deal with in other less successful areas. Such highly successful productive mission partners can often be a prime target for attack by the enemy, and a properly informed PACTeam can be an immense prayer defence.

Remember, *problems arise if you leave your PACTeam 'out in the cold'.*

To think about:

How much initiative would you want your PACTeam to take in keeping in close touch with you and your family?

4. You must not confuse the role of the Agency with the PACTeam.

Remember the basic foundational roles we have already defined: the agency's role is primarily concerned with your 'work'; the PACTeam's role is primarily concerned with you as a person. I recall vividly my early days in cross-cultural work, when the General Secretary of SU India, under whom I worked, expressed his frustration with me when I consistently failed to submit reports and bills on time. This was long before the days of e-mails and I could give any number of excuses. Behind his frustration there probably lurked a suspicion that I disrespected his authority over me. I learnt the hard way to distinguish between accountability for my work, and accountability for my personal life. At that time I did not have a properly formed PACTeam. It was more my family and my fiancé with whom I poured out the 'anguish of my soul' – being a young bachelor far from home, I had plenty of 'anguish'! But now, with Ruthie by my side, and with our PACTeam well established, we still have to constantly remind ourselves and them, where the boundaries lie. Over decades now we have relocated internationally to work in five or six different cultures. On each shift we have become accountable for our work to different people and different agencies. But regardless of our work accountability, we have remained **personally** accountable to our PACTeam, who have remained the same people throughout.

To think about:

How do we maintain a good balance between work and personal accountability?

5. Remember, you as a cross-cultural worker need to 'create the climate' of trust towards your PACTeam – by being accountable!

The concept of being personally accountable to

others is not a common pattern in everyday life. In fact many of us believe that we are only personally accountable to God, and that no one has a right to speak into our lives on personal issues. The whole Western way of life tends towards this attitude of independence, so we have to learn a whole new way of thinking in order to have an effective PACTeam.

You as the cross-cultural worker are in the best position to orientate your PACTeam. You may need to bear this in mind in the selection of your PACTeam members. A balance of business, professional, home-carers, and church leaders will usually help. Your friends may have no experience of cross-cultural work, but you want to demonstrate your trust in them and your willingness to be accountable to them in your personal life. We would like to suggest three simple principles to keep a PACTeam healthy:

- **Assign roles.** Initially, when we first began our PACTeam, we did not assign particular jobs to each. We therefore found that some felt they had very little to do, and others felt overburdened. We soon learnt that it was our responsibility to ensure that all the PACTeam felt needed and valued, and it was not long before our mutual vulnerability to one another ensured that we had sorted that out pretty fast! In hindsight, though, our work was already established. Yours, as you start out, might not yet be. So a smaller and simpler model might suit you well. How about starting with 3 or 4 friends, with the possibility of expansion. Later, as you see the need for different roles, you can specifically assign those and expand your team.

- **Meeting together.** We stress in this book the value of meeting regularly with our PACTeam - at least once a year - and for them to meet at regular intervals throughout the time we are away. However we realise that each PACTeam will be different and yours may be selected from friends who live far apart, maybe even in different continents. The immediacy of Skype and social media and other internet connectors means that your PACTeam may only be able to meet in cyber space! Why not, if that is the best way for you? Meeting in person is special, but if your needs for personal accountability and care can be met over the internet, then feel free to make that possible. Maybe your PACT will be a Personal Accountability Cyber Team!

- **Retiring a PACTeam member.** Not an easy thing to do! As time goes on all our personal situations change and it may be that one of your team feel they need to retire. Let that happen happily. It may be, however, that you feel one of the PACTeam members is being obstructive and you wish them off! We would suggest that you use that as an opportunity to talk frankly and openly together about the 'obstructiveness'. Maybe using the Matt 18 model of speaking one to one first, then if necessary, with another PACTeam member, and then if still necessary to open the whole can of worms to the PACTeam's prayerful and loving decision making. As you are all in a SAFE relationship together, that could be a real-life situation to test your vulnerability and your ability to love and forgive one another. If, after all has been said or done, and the problem is not resolved, we would suggest you disband the PACTeam for a period of time, and then re-start it with a new selection of SAFE friends (see the chapter five, creating your PACTeam).

Regardless of these five pitfalls, and any others you may come across, your PACTeam, fired by the power and encouragement of the Holy Spirit and the fuel of their prayer will keep you going for the long haul. Together we will move forward to fulfil His kingdom shout to "make disciples of all nations".

Afterword

Ross Paterson

The PACTeam is a product of recent technology and mobility. The arrival of the Internet and of swift Wi-Fi and broadband connections has opened up a whole new world. Skype and other cheap telephone calls enable us to talk with friends all over the globe. Alongside that has come cheap travel (at least relatively cheap!) and thus access to most countries in the world. The concepts unpacked in this book only work because this is so.

Whenever the Lord leads us to respond to this kind of innovation, thus opening up new fields of support and service for those of us in global missions, we need simultaneously to avoid two extremes.

We need to be careful that we do not resist God-given innovation. We read, for example, that 100 years ago James O Fraser's prayer support group, led by his mother in the UK, laboured with him in prayer for the Lisu people in SW China amongst whom he was working. Without doubt this small group played a huge part in the revival that eventually broke out – yet more than likely none of them ever even saw a photograph of those they were praying for! Likewise John and Isabel Kuhn, Fraser's successors in the work, saw amazing reconciliation take place between warring factions in a village, only to read in a letter, received two months later, that the breakthrough came at exactly the time when their supporters in Canada were praying! Are we to conclude from these stories that, because the Holy Spirit worked so amazingly through prayer in the absence of modern communications and ease of travel, that we should continue to manage without them now in our generation? Surely not!

At the same time, we also need to be careful that we do not fly in the opposite direction – declaring that all that has gone before is to be discarded, and all that is needed now is a PACTeam! A careful reading of this book will show that that is not what is being said. We firmly believe that the sending church, the agency, team members on the field, as well as national believers – and other provisions of the Lord, like occasional visitors bringing encouragement – can all play a part in providing for global workers' support on the field. But the PACTeam has a crucial role. We are excited by the simplicity and flexibility of this relatively 'new invention'. Try it and see – and encourage others to do the same!

The Lord himself said that the wise teacher should draw from both the old and the new (Matt 13:52). If we heed Him, He will produce for us a new level of service and support for an emerging generation of cross-cultural workers. We shall also, I pray, see more 'all church membership' engagement in the command of the Lord Jesus to reach unto the ends of the earth with His Gospel. I look forward to seeing this in the months and years to come, as PACTeams develop and mature for the Kingdom's sake.

Appendix A - Loading the baskets

Rod and Ruthie Gilbert

Here you will find a set of checklists with ideas for you and your PACTeam.

Prayer	PACTeam member
Receive regular updates	
Send encouragement	
Give specific insight	
Record testimonies and answers to prayer	
Give words of prophecy or scriptures to encourage	
Gather others to intercede	
Manage "hotline" for urgent prayer	
Keep sending church aware of prayer needs	
Arrange half night of prayer together	
Have 24 hours of prayer with all the supporters joining in country wide	
Have a prayer time linking with other PACTeams	
Arrange a children's fun prayer gathering	
Cultural food and prayer event	

Practical help	PACTeam member
Looking after a privately rented house	
Dealing with difficult tenants	
Buying/selling your house	
Finding storage for personal possessions	
Taking care of pets	
Lending you seasonal clothes	
Lending you a house for home visit	
Meeting the children's needs in your absence	
Visiting a sick relative on your behalf	
Arranging for you to hire or borrow a car	
Sending on mail	
Lending you a caravan for a holiday	
Helping with packing up	
Clearing blocked drains and other building maintenance	
Holding clothing for you to use on urgent short visits.	
House cleaning on your departure and before you return.	
Lifts to/from airport	
Holding power of Attorney	

Provision - Fundraising and finance	PACTeam member
Help with planning a budget	
Keeping your financial needs in the minds of your supporters. E.g. fridge magnets, cards, notes, presentations, commitment forms	
Arranging gift days or fund raising events	
Communicating with you about gifts received	
Managing your bank accounts	
Developing a system for tax rebate	
Advising on pensions or insurance schemes	
Sending notes of thanks to donors	
Keeping you up to date with tax situations	
Helping you with your will	
Helping you form a charitable trust	
Sending or visiting with goodies from home	

Pointman – PACTeam coordinator	PACTeam member
Emailing and phoning you and the rest of the team regularly	
Visiting you and reporting back to your PACTeam and supporters	
Arranging when and where the team meets	
Chairing the meeting of the PACTeam	
Being sensitive to the Spirit: giving leadership and friendship to the team	
Anticipating your needs and those of the team, ahead of time	
Being a 'junction box' for information to you and to the team	
Sending out your newsletter (*this may be done by PR*)	
Connecting with your mission agency	
Linking with your sending church and other supporters	

PR- maintaining personal relationships by	PACTeam member
Post	
Email	
Skype	
Social network	
Text	
Phone	
Visits	
Sending birthday gifts	
Remembering important celebrations	
Photos	
Special treat gifts	

Planner (or Prophet!)	PACTeam member
Sending links to pod-casts; web-sites	
Sending magazine articles	
Sending your local magazine or newspaper	
Networking for you with other similar projects or ministries	
Planning your deputation schedule (so you don't burn out)	
Connecting you to further supporting churches	
Booking conferences for input as well as output	
Finding out about medical checks that you may need	

Appendix B - The Biblical precedent of the sending church

- An example to follow

Ross Patterson

The Bible, which is the handbook of cross-cultural work for CCWs, places major responsibility for the Great Commission in the hands of the local church. PACTeams flow out of church life as specialised teams in the same great task. The advantage of PACTeams, and their main reason for existing, is that they give support to the individual CCW – committed, burdened and servant-hearted people who want to ensure that the CCW is being cared for – and clearly knows that is so!

The role of the sending church is thus absolutely critical. Let me outline seven areas that are essential. As you read through the points below, you may say that your church does not give evidence of them, but the point is that Scripture does. So, inasmuch as we are committed to the establishment of PACTeams, we should also be engaged in the battle to see cross cultural work as a 'whole church' activity, not just the involvement of a few people. The danger of a PACTeam is that those who are committed to CCW work disappear from church life and involve themselves in a PACTeam separately. I personally believe that is profoundly unhelpful. We should work to see Biblical patterns established in churches that follow the Scriptures.

Proper Birthing

Taking Paul as our model, in Acts 9, where Paul is wonderfully saved out of hostility to Christianity, he is introduced straight into church life. He is met and wonderfully greeted by Ananias, a church leader. He then wins others into the same family of Christ, the Damascus church (Acts 9:19, 22, 25). This birth process is essential. A Christian who has a healthy church life at once learns how to function in plurality. Once that person has served as a member in the Body of Christ in the early days of Christian experience, then a PACTeam can be extremely helpful in giving support to that individual as he or she goes out. Giving an individual special focus without a corporate church identity can be dangerous.

Building up in the Word

Paul had the opportunity to meet with the leaders in Jerusalem and test out his salvation experience (Acts 9) and then was sent by the church to Tarsus. Interestingly, when Barnabas called him out of Tarsus to join him in Antioch, the function in which both engaged was teaching of the Word (Acts 11:25-26). At the end of Acts 15, other teachers had been raised up, and at that point, when clarity in the Word has been established, Paul was free to move on to the next missionary journey. Establishing a foundation in God's Word through church life is absolutely essential to the CCW. Even with a healthy PACTeam it is too late to try to build this in once the field has been reached.

Definition and Training in Gifts and Calling

Paul had his calling to the Gentile people confirmed at least twice through other church leaders (26:16-18 compare 9:15-16 and 13:1-3). Equally, that year or more spent teaching with Barnabas, the Son of Encouragement, (Acts 11:25-26), changed Paul from a man with Christian blood on his hands into the apostle of grace. Character worked out in church life was an important part of Paul's preparation for his release as a CCW.

Sending

Acts 13 clearly says that Paul was sent out on the first missionary journey, together with Barnabas, through a word that came through church leaders. Church leadership not only authenticated the sending of Paul as a CCW to the Gentiles, but it also laid hands on him, prayed for him, fasted for him and sent him out. The Antioch church leader (Barnabas) actually went with him on the first stage until the end of Acts 15. This model of churches sending out is an absolutely crucial one and the church received them back at the end of Acts 14. Where churches authorise and send, then it is easier for the CCW to be received back. Where that is not so, and perhaps a sub-group has sent or authenticated, there will probably be felt neglect.

Authority and Accountability

It is essential that a CCW has learned to live in the local church, sometimes working under difficult people, and yet accepting the authority that the Lord Jesus has given them – even sometimes when not agreeing with them. That is because later they will face difficulty with relationships on the field. It is often said that the single most common cause of CCWs failing and returning home is conflict on the field. If this has not first been worked out in a position of accountability within the local church, then it is doubtful that they will survive in a cross-cultural situation. Paul was sent by the Jerusalem church back to Tarsus in Acts 9. It is highly doubtful that this was a strategic move – because sending him home to Tarsus took him away from his calling to reach to the Gentiles (compare Paul's statement of ultimate cross-cultural values in Romans 15:16-19, where he yearns to go where the gospel had not been preached)! He stayed in Tarsus until Barnabas, also named as an apostle from Jerusalem, came and rescued him in Acts 11. We often underestimate the sense of authority and accountability that Paul had towards the Jerusalem leaders, even though at times he entirely disagreed with some of them over Gentile issues. Acts 15 shows how he and Barnabas went up to meet with them, even though some had come out from them and caused confusion and disruption in the Antioch church. They did not declare independence, they submitted the issue, and God worked through that accountability. The serious issue here is that in some situations a PACTeam alone will simply not have the stature of leadership to express that accountability in a healthy and Godly way. This can have serious implications to the worker on the field.

Networking

Church life builds into us as believers a sense of

networking. Firstly, a church of any size has different departments, which can compete in terms of resources and people. That forces us to ask whether we are as concerned for other people's ministries as we are for our own, and thus are willing to work with them and even for them. Hopefully, church life will also network much wider than itself, joining together in the Body of Christ. A CCW who cannot network on the field is in serious trouble, and probably will not last long, or will devolve into a lone ranger ministry. If he or she has not learned to network in the church first, then it is doubtful that they will learn once they hit the field with all the cultural issues that they will face.

Resolution

Finally, Acts 15 shows us that church life trains us in how to deal with conflict. As said above, we will face that on the field as CCWs. At the end of Acts 15, Paul and Barnabas have a severe disagreement over John Mark, who departed from them in Acts 13 in an unsatisfactory way. It is interesting that the church in Antioch does not seem to have been rocked by that, and continues with its life, even in the midst of major conflict between its leaders. Of course they had stepped back by Acts 15, so that would have lessened the impact. As stressed in this section, a CCW who cannot handle this type of situation will probably have a short shelf-life. The problem here with a PACTeam is that the members will not be aware of the real nature of the issue, and will instinctively seek to support and set in concrete the response and attitudes of their CCW. Their identification and love of the CCW will almost certainly cause them to get it wrong. In a serious situation, the leadership on the field should have the right to go to the church leadership to work out the steps to be followed, by presenting a much broader report of the events.

Wherever such a church, or a group of churches, exist, a PACTeam can flow out of them in an extremely healthy and productive way. As has been repeatedly emphasised, the members of the PACTeam, whilst enjoying a normal and profitable church life, can at the same time in the PACTeam focus on an individual. Normally a church cannot do this. The church must consider equally the needs for prayer and finance and well-being of all its cross-cultural workers. This combination of local church and PACTeam is an extremely healthy expression of support for the cross-cultural worker.

Other titles by the same authors available from Amazon

Marriage Masala, 52 Spices for a healthy marriage by Rod and Ruthie Gilbert

- http://www.amazon.co.uk/Marriage-Masala-Rod-Gilbert/dp/1935614991/ref=sr_1_1?s=books&ie=UTF8&qid=1326483279&sr=1-1

What in the World is God Waiting For? by Ross Paterson
  (Formerly published as the Antioch Factor - and still obtainable as such from Amazon)

- http://www.amazon.co.uk/What-World-God-Waiting-Fulfilment/dp/1852404310/ref=sr_1_1?ie=UTF8&qid=1326211060&sr=8-1#reader_1852404310

The Continuing Heartcry for China by Ross Paterson

- http://www.amazon.co.uk/Continuing-Heartcry-China-Ross-Paterson/dp/1852402687/ref=sr_1_1?s=books&ie=UTF8&qid=1326211295&sr=1-1

Printed in Great Britain
by Amazon

65291351R00071